Learn & Play

Sudoku
for Third Grade

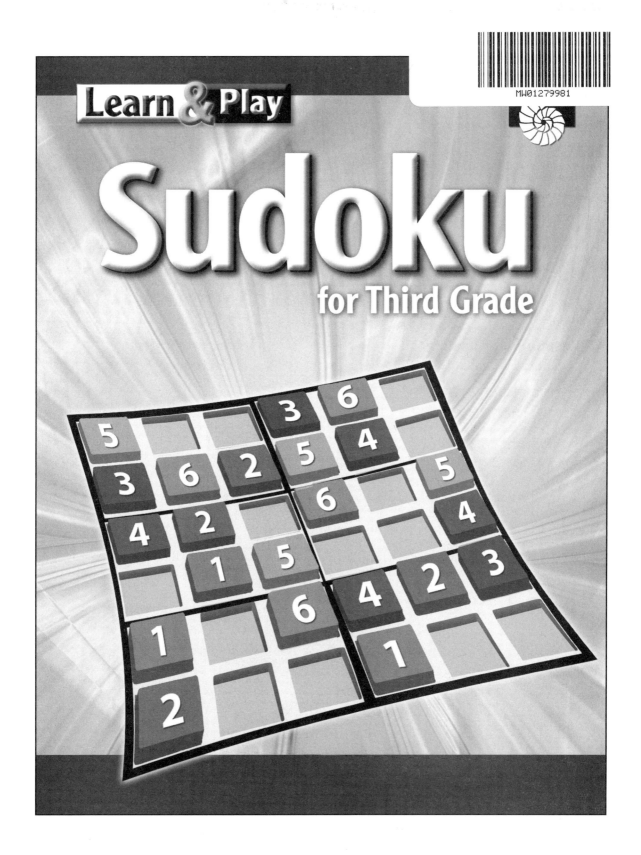

Author

Donna Erdman, M.Ed.

SHELL EDUCATION

Credits

Editorial Product Manager
Karie Feldner Gladis, M.S.Ed.

Assistant Editor
Torrey Maloof

Editorial Assistant
Kathryn R. Kiley

Editorial Director
Emily R. Smith, M.A.Ed.

Editor-in-Chief
Sharon Coan, M.S.Ed.

Editorial Manager
Gisela Lee, M.A.

Creative Director
Lee Aucoin

Cover Designer
Lesley Palmer

Illustration Manager
Timothy J. Bradley

Print Production
Phil Garcia
Don Tran

Interior Layout Designer
Robin Erickson

Publisher

Corinne Burton, M.A.Ed.

Shell Education

5301 Oceanus Drive
Huntington Beach, CA 92649-1030

http://www.shelleducation.com

ISBN 978-1-4258-0322-3

© 2007 Shell Education

Table of Contents

What Is Sudoku?

Whether you are traveling or just relaxing on a Sunday morning, Sudoku is a pastime that the whole family can enjoy. The Sudoku craze has taken over. It is goodbye to crossword puzzles and magic squares. If you search the word *Sudoku* on Google™, you will get over 70 million hits. Sudoku puzzles are published in newspapers, magazines, and books. They even come in electronic handheld games or interactive games on the Web.

Source: TheSupe87/Shutterstock, Inc.

Sudoku is a logic puzzle. Each puzzle has one or more mini-grids. Each mini-grid has boxes that are arranged in rows and columns. Hints are given in some of the boxes. There are different types of puzzles. The puzzles can be 1 x 1 grids, 2 x 2 grids, 2 x 3 grids, 3 x 3 grids, or even more. Pictures, letters, and numbers are all used within the puzzles in this series.

The objective of a Sudoku puzzle is to fill in all the boxes of the puzzle using only the given hints. Each column, row, and mini-grid must have each picture, letter, or number only once. That means you have to pay attention to three things while you try to solve these puzzles. You have to look up and down the column, across the row, and around the mini-grid!

The History of Sudoku

How did the Sudoku craze start? Sudoku puzzles first appeared in a U.S. magazine in 1979. At that time it was called "number place." A magazine editor from Japan saw the number place puzzle and liked it so much that he decided to create a magazine with his version of it. He called the puzzle Sudoku. The word *su* in Japanese means *number,* and the word *doku* means *single.* The puzzle became very popular in Japan. Today, 660,000 Sudoku magazines are circulated every month in Japan.

Source: Daniel Gale/Shutterstock, Inc.

The Sudoku craze spread to the United Kingdom when Wayne Gould saw the puzzle in a magazine while working in Hong Kong. He was fascinated by the puzzles, so he created a computer program to generate Sudoku puzzles. Then, he sold his idea to the *London Times.* They used Gould's program to create a series for their daily games pages. Other newspapers then jumped on the bandwagon, spreading the craze back to the United States. In April 2005, Sudoku became a regular feature in the *New York Post. The Daily News* and *USA Today* followed a few months later.

The History of Sudoku *(cont.)*

Deep Roots

The puzzle goes back further than 1979. It actually has its roots in Latin Squares. Latin Squares were taken from the work of Swiss mathematician Leonhard Euler. He lived from 1707 to 1783. A Latin Square is a square grid that contains sets of different symbols repeated. The cells of the grid contain each symbol only once and the symbol can appear only once in each row and column. (Sound familiar?) Sudoku puzzles are really Latin Squares that have some of the symbols already filled in, and you have to fill in the rest. A set of Latin Squares is combined to form a Sudoku puzzle.

Portrait by Johann Georg Brucker

A Mental Sport

In 2006, the World Puzzle Federation held its first World Sudoku Championship. Like the Olympics, different countries send teams. There are both individual and team competitions. Each country can enter six participants plus one nonplaying captain. The participants have to solve different variations of Sudoku puzzles.

Find Out More

- What other number puzzles have similar rules to Sudoku?
- What other ideas have come from mathematician Leonhard Euler?

Sudoku Research

Sudoku is a kind of logic puzzle. No mathematical skills are needed to solve the puzzles, and you do not even need to use arithmetic. People solve the puzzles by logical reasoning alone (Sharp 2006). For this reason, these puzzles can be interesting and addictive for both children and adults alike. Not only are the puzzles a fun hobby, but the skills used to solve Sudoku puzzles can be transferred and applied to other areas of life.

For young people, the main benefit of solving Sudoku puzzles is the development of logical reasoning skills. These skills will help them solve math problems.

> There is a misconception that logical reasoning has nothing to do with mathematics. This seems to be tied to the idea that mathematics is about numbers. Indeed, Sudoku puzzles could have letters or colors or pictures instead of the numbers or any other property that comes with various attributes. (Sharp 2006)

Sudoku Research *(cont.)*

The heart of the puzzle, the mini-grid, is really a math problem about arrangements or combinations of objects (Sharp 2006). Logic is required in most areas of mathematics, and many examples of math problems can be given that require logical reasoning. Students can also use logical reasoning skills to find new ways to look at a problem and develop creative problem solving strategies.

To fully understand the depth of math concepts and become lifelong learners of mathematics, students need both logical reasoning and problem-solving skills. By solving Sudoku puzzles, students will begin to develop systematic thinking. They will learn to identify patterns and apply them. And, they will develop an awareness of the need to examine data carefully. These skills will also transfer over to other content areas, such as language acquisition. Puzzles are "well suited for contributing to a problem-based environment that is conducive to learning in the second-language classroom and may play an important role in the development of critical and higher-order thinking skills." Most importantly, puzzles offer second-language students the opportunity to repeat vocabulary and sentence structures in authentic contexts (Raizen 1999).

In the classroom, Sudoku puzzles are an easy way to differentiate instruction. The different grade levels of Sudoku can be used in one classroom. Each student can be given a puzzle from the grade level and skill level that bests suits his or her cognitive development of logical reasoning and problem-solving skills.

> Riddles and puzzles have broad appeal and are accessible to literally all ability levels. The conditions and objectives of the problems that are posed as puzzles are usually understood easily, although the solutions may be challenging. Even though some students may not be able to solve every puzzle, many enjoy the challenge of the attempt. (Evered 2001)

Students who have not been successful in mathematics can find success in solving Sudoku puzzles. In the preface to Raymond Smullyan's book, *The Lady or the Tiger and Other Logic Puzzles*, he states, "So many people I have met claim to hate math, and yet are enormously intrigued by any logic or math problem I give them, provided I present it in the form of a puzzle. I would not be at all surprised if good puzzle books prove to be one of the best cures for the so called, math anxiety" (1982).

Sudoku puzzles serve as an excellent warm-up activity, closing activity, problem-of-the day, enrichment activity, or break from the traditional curriculum content. Will Shortz, a puzzle creator and editor, states, "You can learn it in 10 seconds, and yet the logic needed to solve Sudoku is challenging. It's a perfect amount of time to spend on a puzzle, anywhere from five minutes to half an hour" (Bennett 2006).

Sudoku Research *(cont.)*

The puzzles are engaging and addictive for students. Filling in the empty cells appeals to them, and the rush at the very end to complete the puzzle gives them a great feeling of accomplishment. This inherent element of solving the puzzle adds a level of excitement to the classroom and is an intrinsic motivator for students (Evered 2001). The puzzle serves as a catalyst for learning (Raizen 1999).

Source: Ramon Berk/Shutterstock, Inc.

For both adults and students, Sudoku is a way to sharpen your brain and improve your focus. It requires concentration, patience, and self-discipline. According to Shortz, "You have to be focused to be a good Sudoku solver, because if you make a mistake and then base further logic on the mistake you made you have no option but to erase everything and start over. So Sudoku really teaches you to be careful" (Bennett 2006). Sudoku can also be a way to reduce stress or anxiety. While working on the puzzle, all other challenges and worries can be put aside. The puzzle becomes your focus and as a result, your brain feels refreshed and ready to tackle whatever life throws at you. Other researchers are finding Sudoku as a way to slow the progress of Alzheimer's disease (Critser 2006).

This puzzle with its simple rules and small numbers can be a tool for students, teachers, and parents. For students, it helps them develop logical reasoning skills and problem-solving strategies. Students will become self-disciplined, patient, and careful problem solvers. For teachers, it is a tool for differentiating instruction, engaging students, and supporting language acquisition. For parents, it is a family pastime that reduces stress, increases focus, and turns a child from a math hater to a math lover.

Works Cited

Bennett, J. 2006. Addicted to Sudoku. An interview with Will Shortz. *Newsweek* (Society, Web Exclusive), February 23.

Critser, G. 2006. Changing minds in Alzheimer's research. *Los Angeles Times*, November 5.

Evered, L. J. 2001. Riddles, puzzles, and paradoxes. *Mathematics Teaching in the Middle School* 6 (8): 458–461.

Raizen, E. 1999. Liar or truth-teller? Logic puzzles in the foreign-language classroom. *Texas Papers in Foreign Language Education* 4 (n1): 39–50.

Sharp, J. 2006. International perspectives, beyond Su Doku. *Mathematics Teaching in the Middle School* 12 (3): 165–169.

Smullyan, R. 1982. *The Lady or the Tiger and Other Logic Puzzles*. New York: Alfred Knopf.

Introduction

Learn to Play Sudoku

Sudoku Words

- **items**—the pictures, letters, or numbers in the cells of the puzzle
- **mini-grid**—group of square cells that make a large square or rectangle
- **column**—line of cells that go up and down
- **row**—line of cells that go side to side
- **hints**—cells that are filled in before you start the puzzle
- **scanning**—looking at the mini-grids, columns, and rows to find cells with only one possibility for the missing item

Sudoku Rules

- Every mini-grid must have one each of each item.
- Every column must have one each of each item.
- Every row must have one each of each item.

The Parts of a Sudoku Puzzle

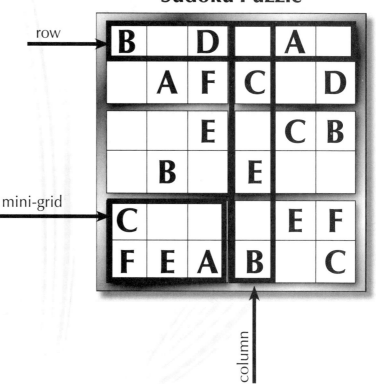

How to Play

- **Step 1**—Look at the puzzle. Find a mini-grid that has lots of hints.
- **Step 2**—Look at each row and column. Fill in the missing items. Each item can only be once in each row or column!
- **Step 3**—Look at the columns and rows again. Check to make sure none of the items are the same. Move any that are repeated.
- **Step 4**—Repeat these steps for each mini-grid.

Top Secret Tip

Try this! Don't look for the mini-grid with the most hints. Look for the column or row with the most hints. Then start the puzzle there.

Strategies for Sudoku

What Is a Strategy?

A strategy is a plan, or a way to solve a puzzle. It is a good idea to have a plan when you're trying to solve math puzzles! That way, you know what steps to take as you work. Strategies definitely help you with Sudoku puzzles. Without a strategy, you may work really hard and still not be able to solve the puzzle. With a plan, you know what steps to take to work through the puzzle.

Strategy 1—Use a Puzzle Blocker

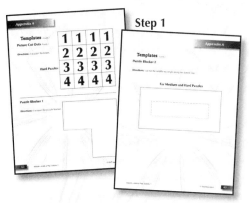

Step 1

- Cut out the Puzzle Blocker on page 63.

Step 2

- Put the Puzzle Blocker across the puzzle.
- You want the top row to show.

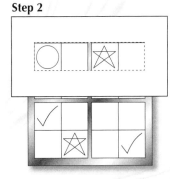

Step 3

- Fill in the empty cells in the row you can see. Make sure you use a pencil because you may have to erase.
- Remove the Puzzle Blocker.

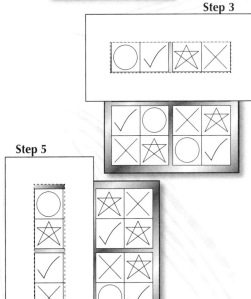

Step 4

- Check the pictures, letters, or numbers. Make sure there is only one of each in each mini-grid.
- If the items are repeated, change them in the row.

Step 5

- Turn the Puzzle Blocker and place it on the far left-hand column.
- Check the items written in the first column. Make sure there is only one of each in the column.
- If the items are repeated, change them in the column.

Step 6

- Move the Puzzle Blocker to the next column and make sure no items are repeated.
- Continue to move the Puzzle Blocker over each column. Check for repeated items in each column.

Step 7

- Place the Puzzle Blocker over the second row and fill in empty cells.
- Then repeat steps 4–6.
- After filling in the empty cells in each row, remove the puzzle blocker. Check each mini-grid, column, and row.

Introduction

Strategies for Sudoku *(cont.)*

Step 1

- Find the mini-grid with the most hints. Ask, "What pictures, letters, or numbers are missing from the mini-grid?"
- Write those missing items outside the mini-grid. These are the only items needed to complete this mini-grid.
- If there is only one empty cell, fill in the missing item and go to another mini-grid.
- If there is more than one empty cell, go to step 2.

Step 2

- Look at a row of the puzzle that crosses the mini-grid from step 1.
- In each empty cell, write any items that are missing in both the mini-grid and the row. Use the list you wrote outside the mini-grid.
- If there is only one possible item left for a cell, fill in the cell with that item.
- If there is more than one possible item, go to step 3.

Step 3

- Repeat step 2 for each row of the puzzle that crosses the mini-grid.
- Move onto step 4 if there are still empty cells in the mini-grid.

Step 4

- Look at a column of the puzzle that crosses the mini-grid from step 1.
- In some of the cells, there will be numbers written from steps 2–3. Cross out any items that are already given in that column.
- If there is only one possible item left for a cell, fill in the cell with that item.
- If there is more than one possible item, go to step 5.

Step 5

- Repeat step 4 for each column of the puzzle that crosses the mini-grid.
- Move onto step 6 if there are still empty cells in the mini-grid that can be filled in with more than one possible item.

Step 6

- Repeat steps 2–5 for all the other mini-grids in the puzzle.
- If you have done all this scanning and still have empty cells, you may have to make an educated guess for one cell. Then, repeat steps 2–5.

Step 1

Steps 2–4

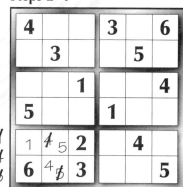

How to Use This Book

Leveled Puzzles

Beginning

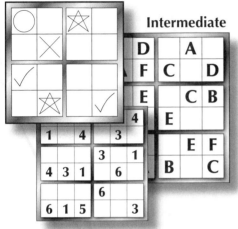

Intermediate

Challenging

- The Sudoku puzzles in this book are divided into three levels: beginning, intermediate, and challenging. Each level has a specific puzzle variation. There are 15 puzzles for each level. That makes a total of 45 puzzles in this book.

- As students move through each level, the puzzles get more difficult. When math teachers created these puzzles, they progressively decreased the number of hints within each variation. They also analyzed the difficulty of each puzzle by the types of logic needed to solve it. Puzzle solvers solved the puzzles to ensure there was one correct solution for each puzzle. In addition, each level of *Learn & Play: Sudoku* was field tested in classrooms.

Themes of Puzzles

- Each of the three levels has a content-area theme tied to state and national standards. The beginning puzzles have a science theme. The intermediate puzzles have a math theme, and the challenging puzzles have a social studies theme.

- All the math themes are tied to the Curriculum Focal Points as identified by the National Council of Teachers of Mathematics.

- Throughout each section, the titles, images, and captions relate to the theme.

Special Additions

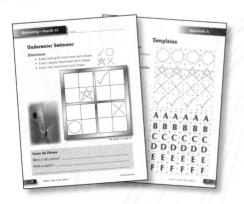

- Special additions are included within each section of puzzles. Some pages have fun facts related to the images. On other pages, students get to write their own fun facts. The last five puzzles in each section show close-ups of pictures. Students should guess what the picture is and write a new caption.

- The appendices include templates, a list of photograph sources, and the answer key. The answer key shows the completed puzzles for your reference.

Introduction

Puzzle Variations at Each Grade Level

	Easy or Beginner		Medium or Intermediate		Hard or Challenging	
	Variation	Hints	Variation	Hints	Variation	Hints
First Grade	1 x 1 with pictures	3–1	2 x 2 with pictures	11–8	2 x 2 with numbers	8–5
Second Grade	2 x 2 with pictures	11–8	2 x 2 with numbers	7–5	2 x 2 with letters	6–4
Third Grade	2 x 2 with pictures	6–4	2 x 3 with letters	20–18	2 x 3 with numbers	17–14
Fourth Grade	2 x 3 with letters	17–15	2 x 3 with numbers	15–13	3 x 3 with numbers	44–40
Fifth Grade	2 x 3 with numbers	12–10	3 x 3 with letters	40–36	3 x 3 with numbers	36–32

Correlations

The activities in this book meet the following standards:

- Students understand and apply basic principles of logic and reasoning.
- Students effectively use mental processes that are based on identifying similarities and differences.
- Students apply basic trouble-shooting and problem-solving techniques.
- Students apply effective decision-making techniques.
- Students use trial and error and the process of elimination to solve problems.

Copyright 2004 McREL. www.mcrel.org/standards-benchmarks.

A correlation of these standards for your state can be printed directly from the Shell Education website: **http://www.shelleducation.com**. If you require assistance in printing correlation reports, please contact Customer Service at 1-800-877-3450.

Oceans

Name _____

High Jump!

Directions

- Every mini-grid must have each shape.
- Every column must have each shape.
- Every row must have each shape.

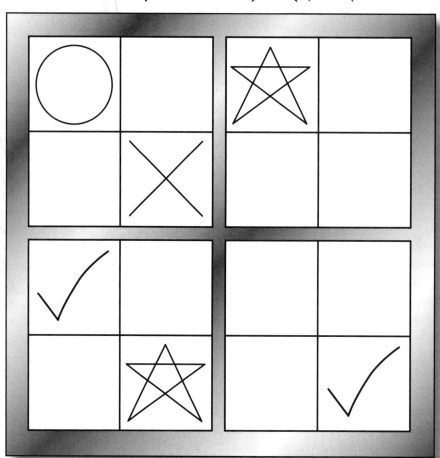

The answer is on page 65.

Dolphins jump high
out of the water.

Yellow Fish

Directions

- Every mini-grid must have each shape.
- Every column must have each shape.
- Every row must have each shape.

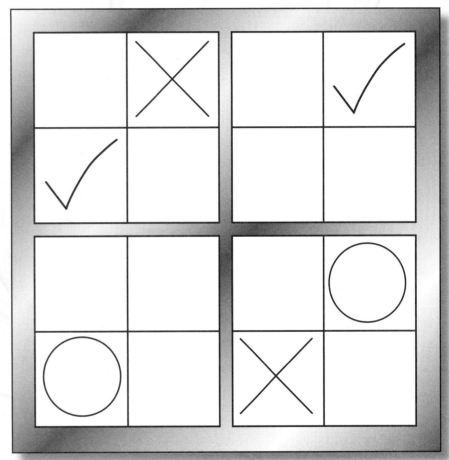

The answer is on page 65.

These fish are swimming near a coral reef.

Name _____

Beware!

Directions

- Every mini-grid must have each shape.
- Every column must have each shape.
- Every row must have each shape.

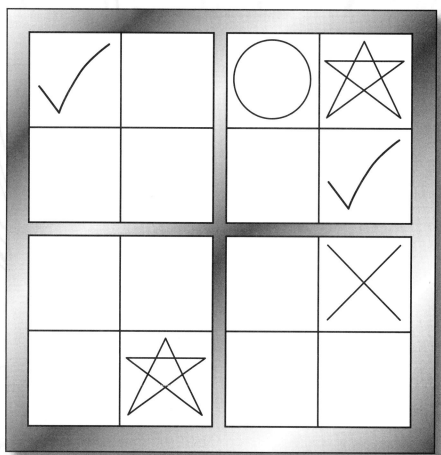

The answer is on page 65.

Sharks are easy to identify because of their sharp fins.

Name _____

Lazy Day

Directions

- Every mini-grid must have each shape.
- Every column must have each shape.
- Every row must have each shape.

The answer is on page 65.

This lobster looks like it's sunning itself on a rock.

Name _____

Gentle Waves

Directions

- Every mini-grid must have each shape.
- Every column must have each shape.
- Every row must have each shape.

The answer is on page 65.

When waves roll into shore, they often carry seashells.

#50322—Learn & Play: Sudoku 3

Name _____

White Whale

Directions

- Every mini-grid must have each shape.
- Every column must have each shape.
- Every row must have each shape.

Beluga whales are easy to identify because they have white skin.

The answer is on page 65.

Whales have the largest brains of any animal. Some people think they are very smart.

Name _____

Staying Warm

Directions

- Every mini-grid must have each shape.
- Every column must have each shape.
- Every row must have each shape.

Mother and baby
sea lions look
happy to be
snuggling.

The answer is on page 66.

Write your own fun fact: _____

_____

#50322—Learn & Play: Sudoku 3

Name _____

Beautiful Coral

Directions

- Every mini-grid must have each shape.
- Every column must have each shape.
- Every row must have each shape.

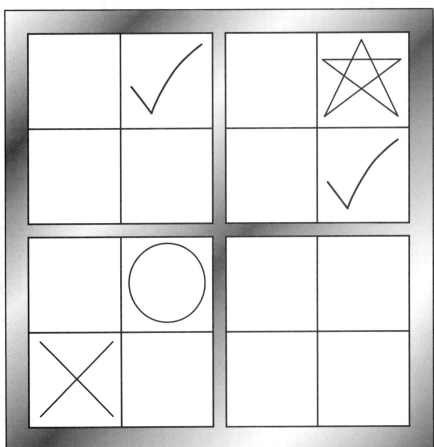

Coral reefs are made up of living organisms.

The answer is on page 66.

Coral reefs offer protection and shelter for many kinds of fish.

Name _____

Sleeping Sea Cow

Directions

- Every mini-grid must have each shape.
- Every column must have each shape.
- Every row must have each shape.

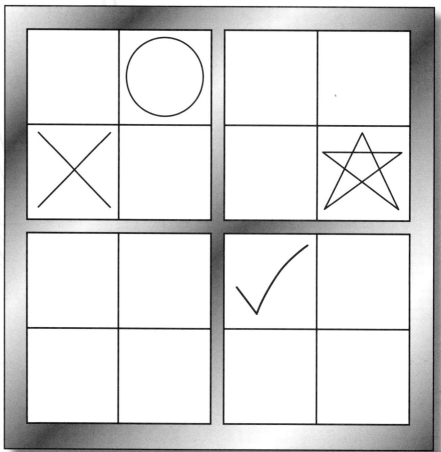

The answer is on page 66.

This manatee is resting on a rock underwater.

One of the biggest dangers to manatees is being hit by boats.

Name _____

Good Eating

Directions

- Every mini-grid must have each shape.
- Every column must have each shape.
- Every row must have each shape.

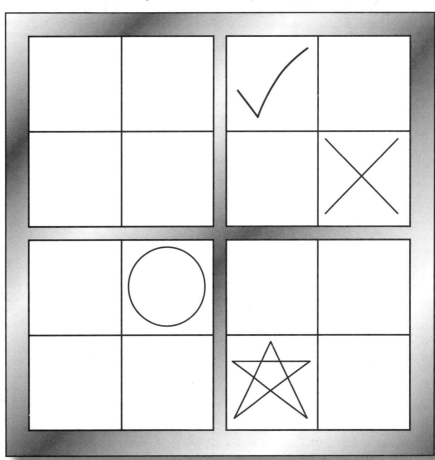

The answer is on page 66.

Crabs caught in the ocean are for sale in a market.

Write your own fun fact:_____

_____

Name _____

Hiding Place

Directions

- Every mini-grid must have each shape.
- Every column must have each shape.
- Every row must have each shape.

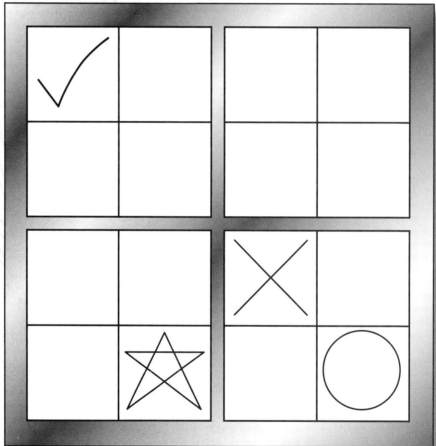

The answer is on page 66.

Guess the Picture

What is this picture? _____

Write a caption: _____

_____

 #50322—*Learn & Play: Sudoku 3*

Name _____

Danger in the Water

Directions

- Every mini-grid must have each shape.
- Every column must have each shape.
- Every row must have each shape.

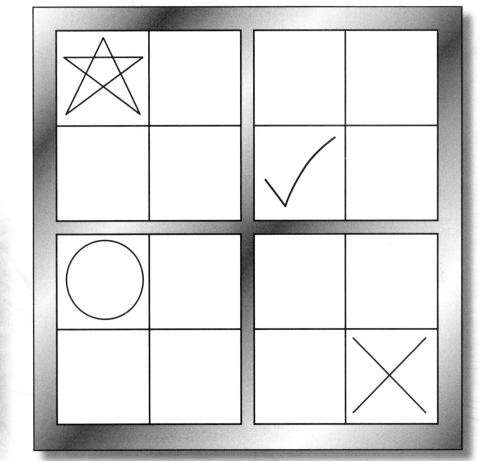

The answer is on page 66.

Guess the Picture

What is this picture? _____

Write a caption: _____

_____

Name _____

Seafood

Directions

- Every mini-grid must have each shape.
- Every column must have each shape.
- Every row must have each shape.

The answer is on page 67.

Guess the Picture

What is this picture? _____

Write a caption: _____

_____

Name _____

Water Lover

Directions

- Every mini-grid must have each shape.
- Every column must have each shape.
- Every row must have each shape.

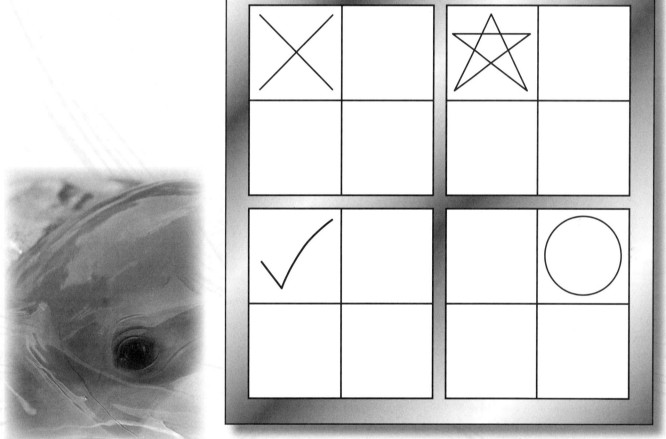

The answer is on page 67

Guess the Picture

What is this picture? _____

Write a caption: _____

_____

Name _____

Underwater Swimmer

Directions

- Every mini-grid must have each shape.
- Every column must have each shape.
- Every row must have each shape.

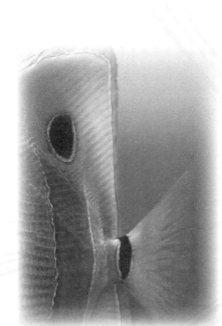

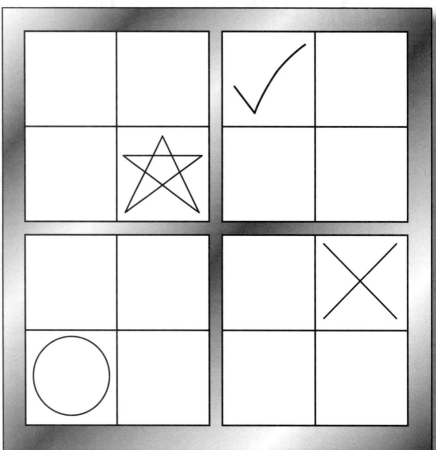

The answer is on page 67.

Guess the Picture

What is this picture? _____

Write a caption: _____

_____

Fractions

Name _____

I'd Like Some Cake, Please

Directions

- Every mini-grid must have each of the letters A–F.
- Every column must have each of the letters A–F.
- Every row must have each of the letters A–F.

B		D		A	
	A	F	C		D
		E		C	B
	B		E		
C				E	F
F	E	A	B		C

The answer is on page 67.

About one quarter
of the cake has
been sliced.

Tick Tock

Directions

- Every mini-grid must have each of the letters A–F.
- Every column must have each of the letters A–F.
- Every row must have each of the letters A–F.

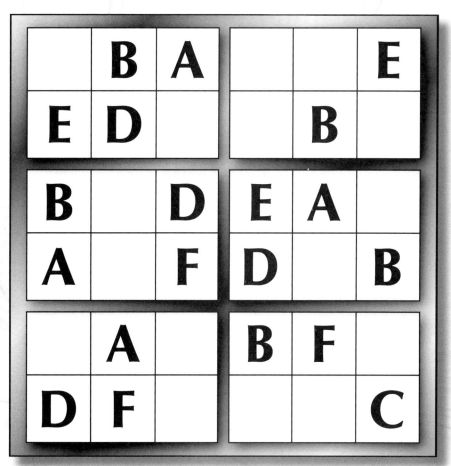

The answer is on page 67.

Clocks divide time into smaller sections called minutes and seconds.

Name _____

Gallon Versus Quart

Directions

- Every mini-grid must have each of the letters A–F.
- Every column must have each of the letters A–F.
- Every row must have each of the letters A–F.

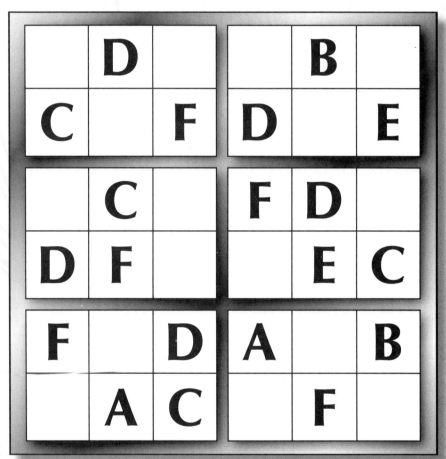

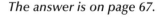

The answer is on page 67.

The smaller bottle of milk is $\frac{1}{4}$ the size of the bigger bottle.

Name _____

Inching Along

Directions

- Every mini-grid must have each of the letters A–F.
- Every column must have each of the letters A–F.
- Every row must have each of the letters A–F.

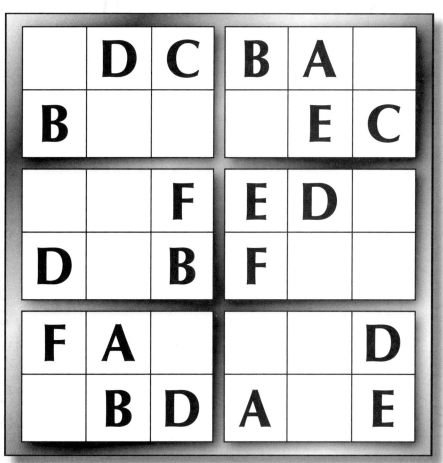

The answer is on page 68.

An inch is $\frac{1}{12}$ of a foot, and a foot is $\frac{1}{3}$ of a yard.

Name _____

Cup of Milk

Directions

- Every mini-grid must have each of the letters A–F.
- Every column must have each of the letters A–F.
- Every row must have each of the letters A–F.

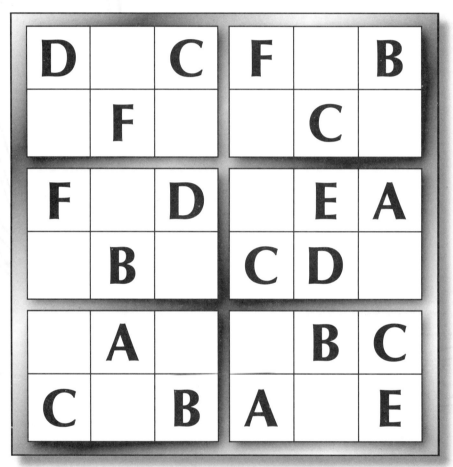

The answer is on page 68.

This measuring container is $\frac{1}{2}$ full with milk.

Yummy in My Tummy

Directions

- Every mini-grid must have each of the letters A–F.
- Every column must have each of the letters A–F.
- Every row must have each of the letters A–F.

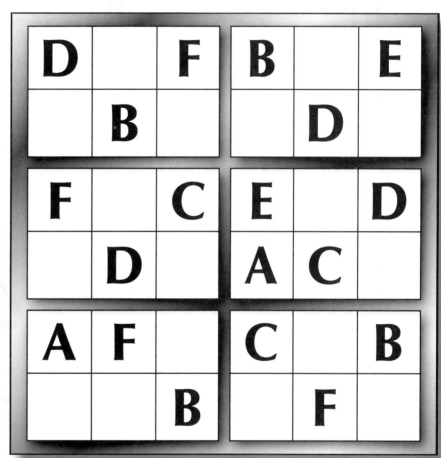

This pizza has been sliced into six pieces of equal size.

The answer is on page 68.

The first pizzeria opened in Naples, Italy, in 1830 and is still open today.

Name _____

Time Flies!

Directions

- Every mini-grid must have each of the letters A–F.
- Every column must have each of the letters A–F.
- Every row must have each of the letters A–F.

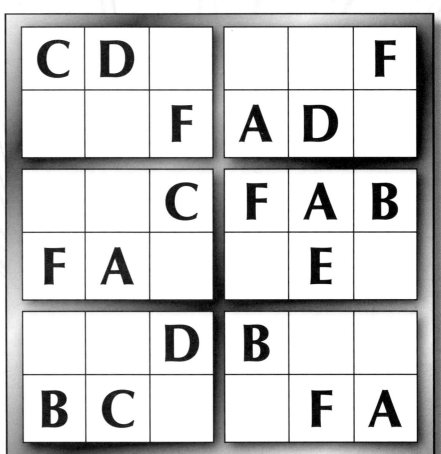

One day is about $\frac{1}{30}$ of a month.

The answer is on page 68.

Calendars were first developed based on the cycles of the sun and the moon.

Kitchen Helper

Directions

- Every mini-grid must have each of the letters A–F.
- Every column must have each of the letters A–F.
- Every row must have each of the letters A–F.

Kitchen scales tell us the weight of a portion of food.

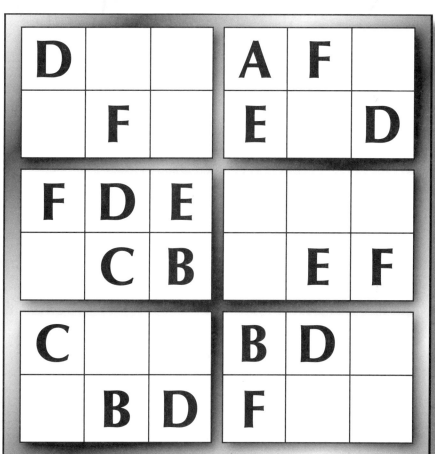

The answer is on page 68.

Write your own fun fact: _____

_____

Name _____

Hike That Ball!

Directions

- Every mini-grid must have each of the letters A–F.
- Every column must have each of the letters A–F.
- Every row must have each of the letters A–F.

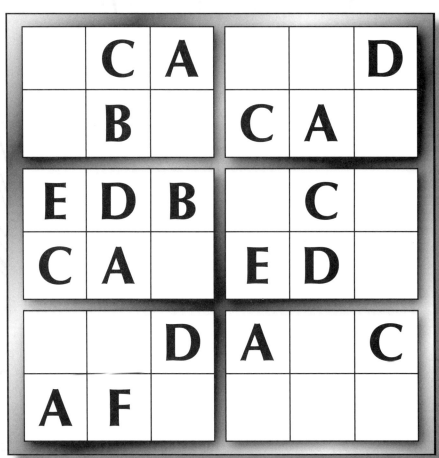

The answer is on page 68.

Ten yards is $\frac{1}{10}$ the length of a football field.

Rutgers University and Princeton University played the first game of college football on November 6, 1869.

Name _____

Change for a Dollar

Directions

- Every mini-grid must have each of the letters A–F.
- Every column must have each of the letters A–F.
- Every row must have each of the letters A–F.

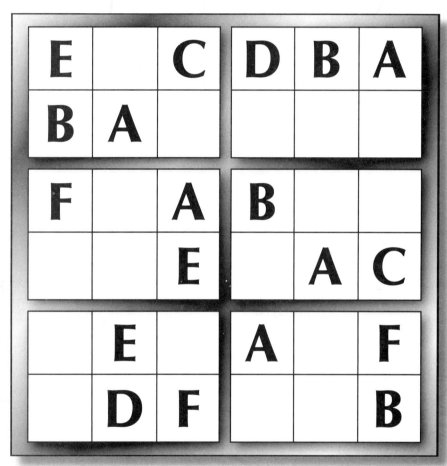

Four quarters equal one dollar.

The answer is on page 69.

Write your own fun fact: _____

_____

Name _____

Tasty Treat

Directions

- Every mini-grid must have each of the letters A–F.
- Every column must have each of the letters A–F.
- Every row must have each of the letters A–F.

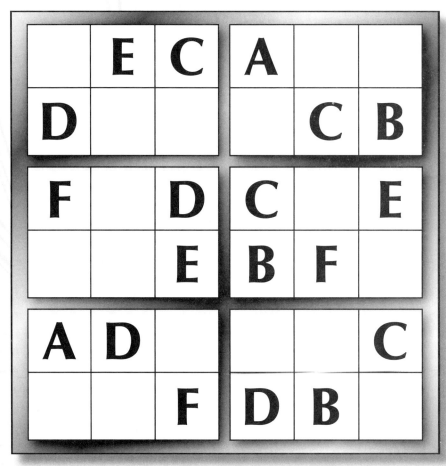

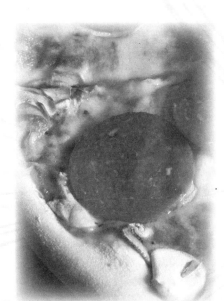

The answer is on page 69.

Guess the Picture

What is this picture? _____

Write a caption: _____

_____

© *Shell Education*

Days and Weeks

Directions

- Every mini-grid must have each of the letters A–F.
- Every column must have each of the letters A–F.
- Every row must have each of the letters A–F.

The answer is on page 69.

Guess the Picture

What is this picture? _____

Write a caption: _____

_____

Name _____

Half a Pint

Directions

- Every mini-grid must have each of the letters A–F.
- Every column must have each of the letters A–F.
- Every row must have each of the letters A–F.

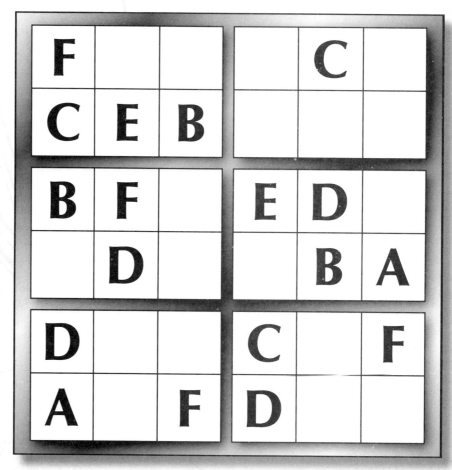

The answer is on page 69.

Guess the Picture

What is this picture? _____

Write a caption: _____

_____

Name _____

Marking Time

Directions

- Every mini-grid must have each of the letters A–F.
- Every column must have each of the letters A–F.
- Every row must have each of the letters A–F.

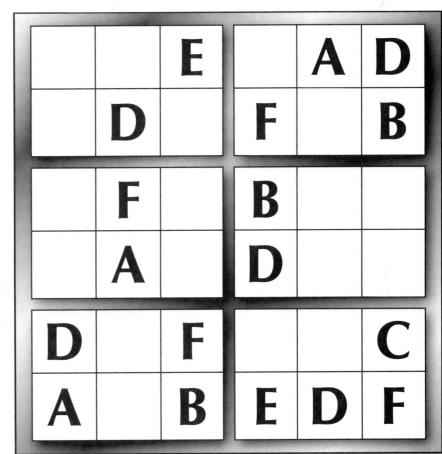

The answer is on page 69.

Guess the Picture

What is this picture? _____

Write a caption: _____

_____

Name _____

Making Change

Directions

- Every mini-grid must have each of the letters A–F.
- Every column must have each of the letters A–F.
- Every row must have each of the letters A–F.

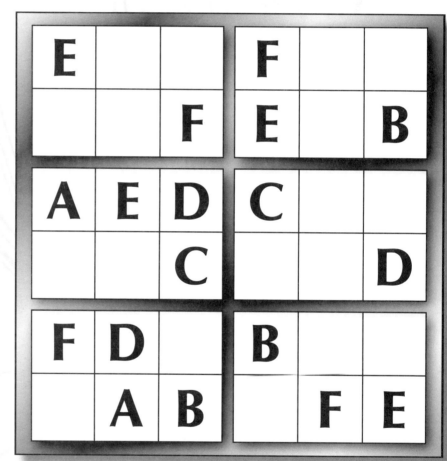

The answer is on page 69.

Guess the Picture

What is this picture? _____

Write a caption: _____

_____

Maps

Name _____

View from the Top

Directions

- Every mini-grid must have each of the numbers 1–6.
- Every column must have each of the numbers 1–6.
- Every row must have each of the numbers 1–6.

2			1		4
1		4		3	
			3		1
4	3	1		6	
			6		
6	1	5			3

The answer is on page 70.

What an interesting view from the top of a globe!

#50322—Learn & Play: Sudoku 3

Name _____

50 States

Directions

- Every mini-grid must have each of the numbers 1–6.
- Every column must have each of the numbers 1–6.
- Every row must have each of the numbers 1–6.

	2				1	
	4	1	3	5	
5		3	4		
2		4	5		3
1					5
4					6

The answer is on page 70.

This map shows the continental United States. It includes 48 of the 50 states. Do you know which two states are missing?

Name _____

Road Trip

Directions

- Every mini-grid must have each of the numbers 1–6.
- Every column must have each of the numbers 1–6.
- Every row must have each of the numbers 1–6.

4		2			6
	5		4		2
	2	4	1	6	
	6			3	
2		5			
1			5	2	3

The answer is on page 70.

A road map shows all the highways on which we can travel.

Name _____

Old Times

Directions

- Every mini-grid must have each of the numbers 1–6.
- Every column must have each of the numbers 1–6.
- Every row must have each of the numbers 1–6.

1	6			5	3
		2	6		
6		5	3		
		1	4		
	1	3	5	4	
4					2

The answer is on page 70.

This map of South
America is over
200 years old.

Name _____

Bird's-Eye View

Directions

- Every mini-grid must have each of the numbers 1–6.
- Every column must have each of the numbers 1–6.
- Every row must have each of the numbers 1–6.

5					3
	2	3	1	6	
	4			1	
	3			5	
	1	2	5	3	
3					1

The answer is on page 70.

Photos taken from airplanes often help when creating maps.

#50322—Learn & Play: Sudoku 3

Name _____

Where Shall We Go?

Directions

- Every mini-grid must have each of the numbers 1–6.
- Every column must have each of the numbers 1–6.
- Every row must have each of the numbers 1–6.

	1		4		5
5					2
4		6		5	
	5		2		
3		1		2	6
2					1

You might find this type of globe in your classroom.

The largest globe is the Unisphere in Queens, New York. It's 12 stories high.

The answer is on page 70.

Name _____

World Wide

Directions

- Every mini-grid must have each of the numbers 1–6.
- Every column must have each of the numbers 1–6.
- Every row must have each of the numbers 1–6.

	4		2	6	
2	5		3		
	6	3			
4		5	1		
		4			1
		2	4	5	

Here's a view of the whole world.

The answer is on page 71.

Every culture in every part of the world uses and makes maps.

#50322—*Learn & Play: Sudoku 3*   © *Shell Education*

Name _____

Bumpy Road

Directions

- Every mini-grid must have each of the numbers 1–6.
- Every column must have each of the numbers 1–6.
- Every row must have each of the numbers 1–6.

A physical map of California and Nevada shows mountain ranges.

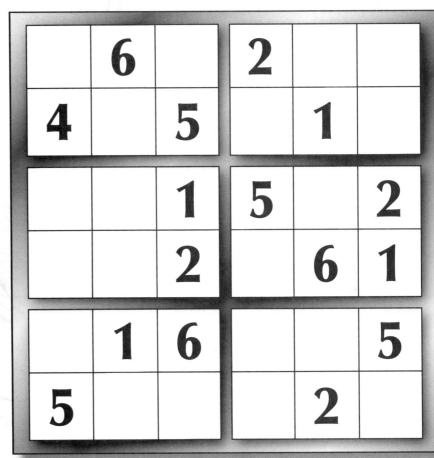

The answer is on page 71.

Write your own fun fact: _____

_____

Name _____

High Winds

Directions

- Every mini-grid must have each of the numbers 1–6.
- Every column must have each of the numbers 1–6.
- Every row must have each of the numbers 1–6.

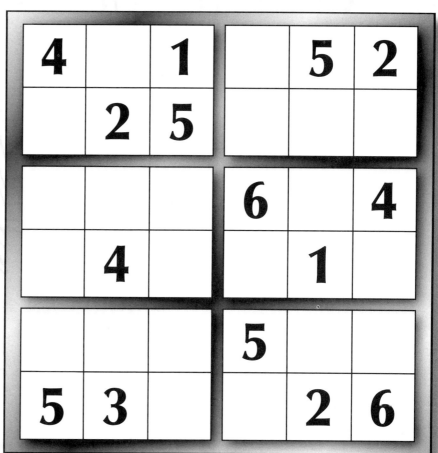

This weather map shows a hurricane over Florida.

The answer is on page 71.

Write your own fun fact:_____

_____

#50322—*Learn & Play: Sudoku 3*
© *Shell Education*

Name _____

Turn Left

Directions

- Every mini-grid must have each of the numbers 1–6.
- Every column must have each of the numbers 1–6.
- Every row must have each of the numbers 1–6.

3		5	1		
	6			2	
6	4				5
2		3		1	4
	3			6	
		6	3		

Global positioning systems guide drivers in the right direction.

The answer is on page 71.

The Global Positioning System (GPS) works by using a network of 24 satellites.

Name _____

Driving Along

Directions

- Every mini-grid must have each of the numbers 1–6.
- Every column must have each of the numbers 1–6.
- Every row must have each of the numbers 1–6.

		4			5
	6	5			3
	4				1
6					
4		3	2		
2			3	5	4

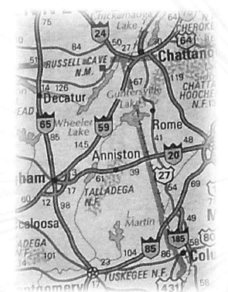

The answer is on page 71.

Guess the Picture

What is this picture? _____

Write a caption: _____

_____

#50322—Learn & Play: Sudoku 3

Many Countries

Directions

- Every mini-grid must have each of the numbers 1–6.
- Every column must have each of the numbers 1–6.
- Every row must have each of the numbers 1–6.

		2	3	1	
5					
1					2
2				4	3
		5		3	1
	4		5		

The answer is on page 71.

Guess the Picture

What is this picture? _____

Write a caption: _____

_____

Small Town

Directions

- Every mini-grid must have each of the numbers 1–6.
- Every column must have each of the numbers 1–6.
- Every row must have each of the numbers 1–6.

3	2	4		6	
		1		4	2
			4		
5				3	1
	1				3
		3	5		

The answer is on page 72.

Guess the Picture

What is this picture? _____

Write a caption: _____

_____

Name _____

Earlier Times

Directions

- Every mini-grid must have each of the numbers 1–6.
- Every column must have each of the numbers 1–6.
- Every row must have each of the numbers 1–6.

4			3		6
	3			5	
		1			4
5			1		
		2		4	
6		3			5

The answer is on page 72.

Guess the Picture

What is this picture? _____

Write a caption: _____

_____

Name _____

Highway Help

Directions

- Every mini-grid must have each of the numbers 1–6.
- Every column must have each of the numbers 1–6.
- Every row must have each of the numbers 1–6.

5			1		
				2	5
		5			2
	6				
4		3	5	1	
	5	6		3	4

The answer is on page 72.

Guess the Picture

What is this picture? _____

Write a caption: _____

_____

Templates

Picture Cut Outs

Directions: Instead of writing the numbers in pencil, use these cutout numbers to fill in the puzzle. Cut out the boxes on the dotted lines. Then place them in the puzzle. You can then move them around on the puzzle until you find all the right spaces!

Beginning Puzzles

Letter Cut Outs

Intermediate Puzzles

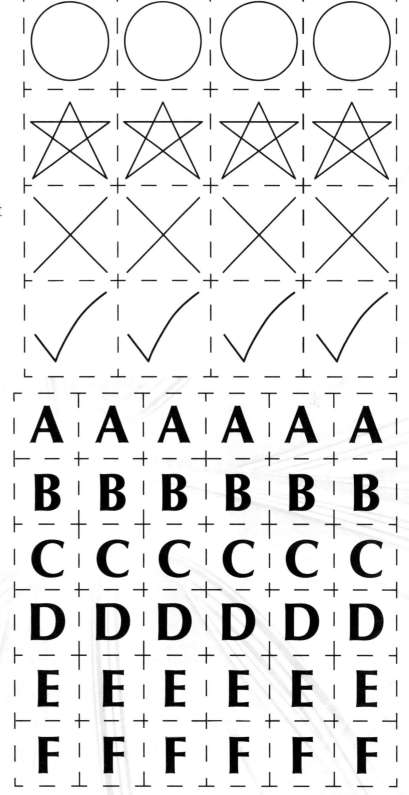

Templates *(cont.)*

Number Cut Outs *(cont.)*

Challenging Puzzles

1	1	1	1	1	1
2	2	2	2	2	2
3	3	3	3	3	3
4	4	4	4	4	4
5	5	5	5	5	5
6	6	6	6	6	6

Templates *(cont.)*

Puzzle Blocker

Directions: Cut out the big rectangle. Then make a window by cutting along the dotted line.

For Beginning Puzzles

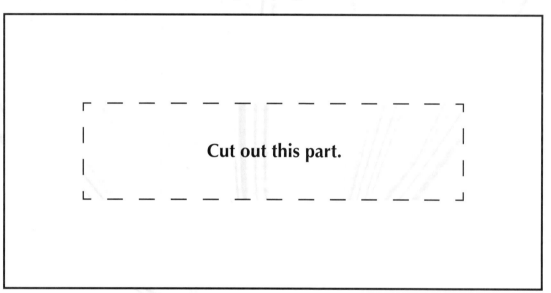

Cut out this part.

For Intermediate and Challenging Puzzles

Cut out this part.

Photograph Sources

Page	Puzzle Title	Photograph Source
14	High Jump!	kristian/Shutterstock, Inc.
15	Yellow Fish	Martin Strmiska/Shutterstock, Inc.
16	Beware!	Ian Scott/Shutterstock, Inc.
17	Lazy Day	Trevor Allen/Shutterstock, Inc.
18	Gentle Waves	coko/Shutterstock, Inc.
19	White Whale	Vlacheslav V. Fedorov/Shutterstock, Inc.
20	Staying Warm	Nik Niklz/Shutterstock, Inc.
21	Beautiful Coral	Martin Strmiska/Shutterstock, Inc.
22	Sleeping Sea Cow	Arrow Studio/Shutterstock, Inc.
23	Good Eating	Stephen Van Horn/Shutterstock, Inc.
24	Hiding Place	Martin Strmiska/Shutterstock, Inc.
25	Danger in the Water	Ian Scott/Shutterstock, Inc.
26	Seafood	Trevor Allen/Shutterstock, Inc.
27	Water Lover	Ferenc Cegledi/Shutterstock, Inc.
28	Underwater Swimmer	Konovalikov Andrey/Shutterstock, Inc.
30	I'd Like Some Cake, Please	Tomo Jesenicnik/Shutterstock, Inc.
31	Tick Tock	Pritmova Svetlana/Shutterstock, Inc.
32	Gallon Versus Quart	Timothy Large/Shutterstock, Inc.
33	Inching Along	Kimberly Hall/Shutterstock, Inc.
34	Cup of Milk	Christopher P. Grant/Shutterstock, Inc.
35	Yummy in My Tummy	Sergey Shandin/Shutterstock, Inc.
36	Time Flies!	Alex Star/Shutterstock, Inc.
37	Kitchen Helper	John Clines/Shutterstock, Inc.
38	Hike That Ball!	Robert Pernell/Shutterstock, Inc.
39	Change for a Dollar	Nikolay Okhitin/Shutterstock, Inc.
40	Tasty Treat	Sergey Shandin/Shutterstock, Inc.
41	Days and Weeks	Alex Star/Shutterstock, Inc.
42	Half a Pint	Christopher P. Grant/Shutterstock, Inc.
43	Marking Time	Ronen/Shutterstock, Inc.
44	Making Change	Sturat Monk/Shutterstock, Inc.
46	View from the Top	Tray Berry/Shutterstock, Inc.
47	50 States	Robert F. Balazick/Shutterstock, Inc.
48	Road Trip	Ingrid E. Stamatson/Shutterstock, Inc.
49	Old Times	Steven Wright/Shutterstock, Inc.
50	Bird's-Eye View	Johnny Lye/Shutterstock, Inc.
51	Where Shall We Go?	Elnur/Shutterstock, Inc.
52	World Wide	Rzymu/Shutterstock, Inc.
53	Bumpy Road	Jason Stitt/Shutterstock, Inc.
54	High Winds	Carolina K. Smith M.D./Shutterstock, Inc.
55	Turn Left	Matt Cooper/Shutterstock, Inc.
56	Driving Along	Ingrid E. Stamatson/Shutterstock, Inc.
57	Many Countries	Elnur/Shutterstock, Inc.
58	Small Town	Johnny Lye/Shutterstock, Inc.
59	Earlier Times	Kenneth V. Pilon/Shutterstock, Inc.
60	Highway Help	Rzymu/Shutterstock, Inc.

Answer Key

High Jump! (page 14)

Yellow Fish (page 15)

Beware! (page 16)

Lazy Day (page 17)

Gentle Waves (page 18)

White Whale (page 19)

Answer Key *(cont.)*

Staying Warm (page 20)

Good Eating (page 23)

Beautiful Coral (page 21)

Hiding Place (page 24)

Sleeping Sea Cow (page 22)

Danger in the Water (page 25)

Answer Key *(cont.)*

Seafood (page 26)

Water Lover (page 27)

Underwater Swimmer (page 28)

I'd Like Some Cake, Please (page 30)

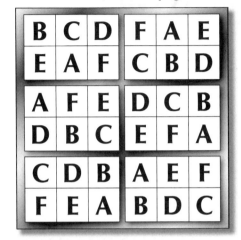

Tick Tock (page 31)

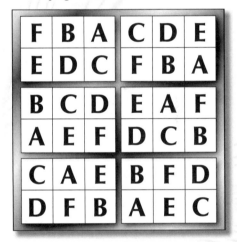

Gallon Versus Quart (page 32)

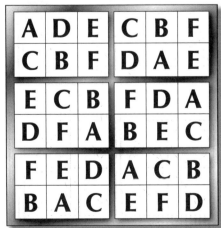

Appendix C

Answer Key (cont.)

Inching Along (page 33)

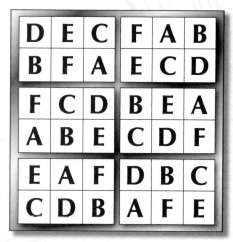

Cup of Milk (page 34)

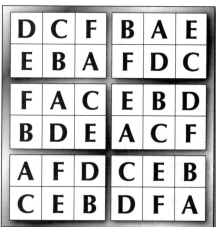

Yummy in My Tummy (page 35)

Time Flies! (page 36)

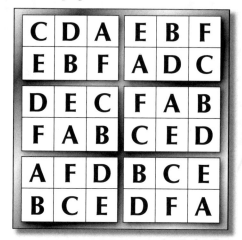

Kitchen Helper (page 37)

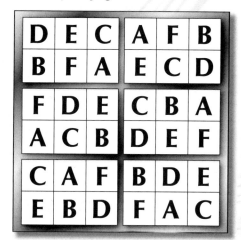

Hike That Ball! (page 38)

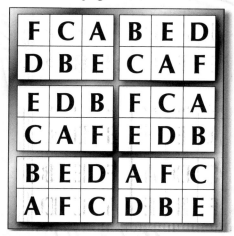

Answer Key *(cont.)*

Change for a Dollar (page 39)

E	F	C	D	B	A
B	A	D	C	F	E
F	C	A	B	E	D
D	B	E	F	A	C
C	E	B	A	D	F
A	D	F	E	C	B

Tasty Treat (page 40)

B	E	C	A	D	F
D	F	A	E	C	B
F	B	D	C	A	E
C	A	E	B	F	D
A	D	B	F	E	C
E	C	F	D	B	A

Days and Weeks (page 41)

B	A	D	C	F	E
E	F	C	D	B	A
D	C	B	E	A	F
A	E	F	B	D	C
C	D	A	F	E	B
F	B	E	A	C	D

Half a Pint (page 42)

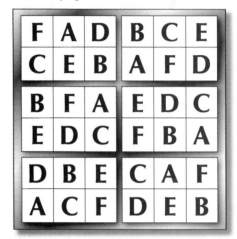

F	A	D	B	C	E
C	E	B	A	F	D
B	F	A	E	D	C
E	D	C	F	B	A
D	B	E	C	A	F
A	C	F	D	E	B

Marking Time (page 43)

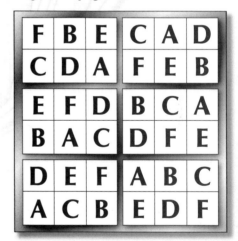

F	B	E	C	A	D
C	D	A	F	E	B
E	F	D	B	C	A
B	A	C	D	F	E
D	E	F	A	B	C
A	C	B	E	D	F

Making Change (page 44)

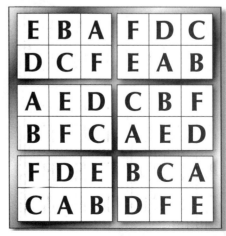

E	B	A	F	D	C
D	C	F	E	A	B
A	E	D	C	B	F
B	F	C	A	E	D
F	D	E	B	C	A
C	A	B	D	F	E

Answer Key (cont.)

View from the Top (page 46)

2	6	3	1	5	4
1	5	4	2	3	6
5	2	6	3	4	1
4	3	1	5	6	2
3	4	2	6	1	5
6	1	5	4	2	3

Old Times (page 49)

1	6	4	2	5	3
5	3	2	6	1	4
6	4	5	3	2	1
3	2	1	4	6	5
2	1	3	5	4	6
4	5	6	1	3	2

50 States (page 47)

3	2	5	6	1	4
6	4	1	3	5	2
5	6	3	4	2	1
2	1	4	5	6	3
1	3	6	2	4	5
4	5	2	1	3	6

Bird's-Eye View (page 50)

5	6	1	2	4	3
4	2	3	1	6	5
2	4	5	3	1	6
1	3	6	4	5	2
6	1	2	5	3	4
3	5	4	6	2	1

Road Trip (page 48)

4	1	2	3	5	6
6	5	3	4	1	2
3	2	4	1	6	5
5	6	1	2	3	4
2	3	5	6	4	1
1	4	6	5	2	3

Where Shall We Go? (page 51)

6	1	2	4	3	5
5	3	4	6	1	2
4	2	6	1	5	3
1	5	3	2	6	4
3	4	1	5	2	6
2	6	5	3	4	1

Answer Key *(cont.)*

World Wide (page 52)

3	4	1	2	6	5
2	5	6	3	1	4
1	6	3	5	4	2
4	2	5	1	3	6
5	3	4	6	2	1
6	1	2	4	5	3

Bumpy Road (page 53)

1	6	3	2	5	4
4	2	5	6	1	3
6	4	1	5	3	2
3	5	2	4	6	1
2	1	6	3	4	5
5	3	4	1	2	6

High Winds (page 54)

4	6	1	3	5	2
3	2	5	4	6	1
1	5	2	6	3	4
6	4	3	2	1	5
2	1	6	5	4	3
5	3	4	1	2	6

Turn Left (page 55)

3	2	5	1	4	6
1	6	4	5	2	3
6	4	1	2	3	5
2	5	3	6	1	4
5	3	2	4	6	1
4	1	6	3	5	2

Driving Along (page 56)

3	2	4	1	6	5
1	6	5	4	2	3
5	4	2	6	3	1
6	3	1	5	4	2
4	5	3	2	1	6
2	1	6	3	5	4

Many Countries (page 57)

4	6	2	3	1	5
5	1	3	2	6	4
1	3	4	6	5	2
2	5	6	1	4	3
6	2	5	4	3	1
3	4	1	5	2	6

Appendix

Answer Key (cont.)

Small Town (page 58)

3	2	4	1	6	5
6	5	1	3	4	2
1	3	2	4	5	6
5	4	6	2	3	1
4	1	5	6	2	3
2	6	3	5	1	4

Earlier Times (page 59)

4	1	5	3	2	6
2	3	6	4	5	1
3	2	1	5	6	4
5	6	4	1	3	2
1	5	2	6	4	3
6	4	3	2	1	5

Highway Help (page 60)

5	4	2	1	6	3
6	3	1	4	2	5
3	1	5	6	4	2
2	6	4	3	5	1
4	2	3	5	1	6
1	5	6	2	3	4

#50322—Learn & Play: Sudoku 3

© Shell Education